dust and conscience

(book of the familiar)

—

Truong Tran

Apogee Press
Berkeley · California
2002

For Marcus, my sister Birtchi! with my fuckin love! ♡

for my mother
and the memory of my father

Grateful acknowledgment is made to the editors of the following journals
and other publications in which parts of this book have appeared or
are scheduled to be published: *Coracle, Transfer, Manoa, Five Fingers Review,
The Battery Review* and the *SFUI Quarterly*.

The Book of Perceptions was first published as a limited edition by
Kearny Street Workshop through a grant from The Creative Work Fund.

Note: The italicized passage, "discus starred with premonitions throw
yourself out of yourself," is from Paul Celan's *Last Poems*.

Book design by Philip Krayna Design, Berkeley, California.
www.pkdesign.net

Cover photograph by Noah David Smith.

ISBN 0-9669937-8-0. Library of Congress Catalog Card Number 2001-135179.

Published by Apogee Press, Post Office Box 8177, Berkeley CA, 94707-8177.
www.apogeepress.com

Table of Contents

—

if only i were a dissident poet i could claim my poems were once written in a cell scraps of paper brought to me by a rat on a string if i wrote about the blue skies would you look up point to god in a pillow of clouds if i wrote about the blinding sun would you stare with faith see for the first time i mean truly see if only i were a dissident poet my name its meaning would i then care to know

· beginnings ·

inception incipience debut dawn where would i begin if not at home to preserve the bitterness he scattered his children in four directions sat back in his chair and proceeded to grow old he waited until the time was right he paid them a visit when they went to kiss their father he licked their skin he found the bitterness still clinging to his tongue he tells his children i want to go home approach it as you will but do so knowing that the line which connects the perceptions to the perceived is crossed with the line of the needs and necessities and there at the crossing are the casualties fragments to stories some still struggling to find the beginnings

hers is a story all too familiar the story of those left behind
fatherless forever searching in an existence where forever is finite
this she tells me is a necessity hers is the story of conflicting
hair disowning her in one culture or another the story of skin
thickened by sun and neglect years upon years hers is the story
of possession a dog tag is no substitute but it will have to do

that in his death we have returned to wade along these flooded
streets to eat of the fruits our tongues have forgotten making
good on the promise made between a father and a son the
beginnings to an end without singularity in such a time in such
a place i think of it as arriving at a context

my lady of the lake with your ebony smile in a past life you lived
as my mother and i your son wandering from market to market
town to town with the weight of dragon fruits on our shoulders
you and i my lady of the lake we are not so different beyond
this threshold of distance and time that an orange is orange
from where i come from this my lady of the lake is but a minor
discrepancy for beyond any threshold is the promise of home

i've located you to a letter in the alphabet do not think it wrong
of me it is by no means a reduction of your being this is done
only so that i may address you free of the inhibitions found in
a name they are temporarily submerged if not discarded let's
say that you are k and i am t removed from our context t met
k in country v t fell in love with both k and v the sum of which
is a language unrequited

she sits in her new car she listens to the cd she is reminded of home she is overwhelmed with sadness she is parked in her garage she is reminded of home i walk these streets as if you were beside me walking step for step the distance of the lake on this given day no giant turtle has emerged from the waters nothing of the fable you've told has fruitioned only the comfort of a satisfying walk a game of badminton to settle the score then and only then would we part you to explore your place of birth and i to find a tranquil moment then and only then would i arrive at your mourning

that series of photos i saw on tv of the one man he was
pointing a gun at the temple of another man had he not pulled
the trigger in that instance of the third frame each decision not
arrived at holds a reality of its own had there been no effect to
document on film to frame and reframe had there been no cause
to arrive at the word war

my father as the scholar instead of the soldier teaching his way towards an early retirement my mother says i would have been married in saigon settled with two children as for that man in the picture holding the gun where would he be now as it is decisions arrived at somewhere in southern california he owns a restaurant i've written a poem it is not that i am forgetful or lazy i have written letters to each and every one of you but i choose not to send them for such an act means that the existence of home would then be confined to one or the other

the lanterns made to usher in the full moon an art form that
dies with the father in a foreign land left intact is the slivering of
bamboo images of the past shelved to collect dust waiting for
rebirth into the familiar as in the shadow that steps into itself
so that the child may emerge whole existing on his own terms

dear suzanne the world here is nothing as we know it i am sitting in a cafe where stools of bamboo make for seats wind as if derived from liquid heat blows at me from all directions the music in the background is prewar french and the women who pass by this cafe window have mastered the art of riding side saddle dodging traffic as predictable as life so you i'm sure can understand it when i say that the world is nothing as i know it and yet i sit at this window as if i were there yes the stories are at times overwhelming but would i stop listening the answer is no for without the stories there would be no history and without the history there would be no people where then would i be if not the acronym the oddity the visitor the native

· perceptions ·

perhaps in another time our story would be different there would be no leaving and thus no returning you would be the teacher in a northern village and i the fisherman we would live quietly to the background singing of cicadas the whispering of the ocean's breath and poems like weeds would grow from the cracks of our lives perhaps in that life the frog and the scorpion are better off as lovers of using words to make concrete the elusive nature of one's identity as if language like glue could piece together the gathered fragments resulting in a form mangled but cohesive weighted it will serve the purpose of anchoring

a waifish young man in a baseball cap cropped hair and knee
torn jeans my taste in men changes with the wind an adams
apple wire rimmed glasses they say girls often marry in the
image of their fathers he is reading whitman better yet celan on
this street a siren screams people rushing to and from their lives
a poem on a panel inside a bus sheds its meaning *discus starred
with premonitions throw yourself out of yourself*

how does one know one knows in the waiting the
imperfections for in a perfect world there is no waiting the
cyclo driver works on a set price at a set time he is at your front
door this of course is with the understanding that he is not
waiting he happens to be in the neighborhood reading a
newspaper finishing his cup of iced coffee in a perfect world
i am thinking of k and he is thinking of me k arrives just as i
arrive as if on cue the three converge together in this perfect
world we are driven k and i

for nothing of the body is inconspicuous staring at my fingers an ant crawling from the index across my palm towards the wrist a perilous journey for my eyes are following its every move a diversion from looking at what is yours is necessary for words like marbles are falling from my lips my father's habit mine to inherit words like i i i want to take you home to my family and their judgments be it good or bad the traditions of dinner a table full of strangers awkward painful family as defined by my mother's darting eyes i want to assure you with calming whispers i think she likes you it is a gradual process she's not much for words like all words meaningless without the context you i this insect fated to a shadow descending for in this instance when skin touches skin the pressures of life will cease to exist

here then is my nature as truthful as can be i sit in a room i have
the music on a single song repeating a study in contradictions
the context in which i meet k consider if you will the likelihood
of a four star hotel amidst the bustling of a third world
cosmopolitan where for the first time i hear this song caught in
between kitsch and camp such is the contradiction of falling
apart before one arrives at falling in love a word both obscene
and sublime by virtue of meaning

that feeling of disdain when you arrive at the conclusion by you i mean i i mean you in return an appropriated word it means going for the first time born in nevada she returns to vietnam describes the people as not pretty but nice a cyclo driver reads shakespeare in translation his latest theory that oj simpson is the modern day othello caliban and ariel are one and the same like a perfect teapot at once awkward yet graceful by design i met a sand crab on a deserted beach and we sat there among the dunes discussing the crab's fortitude i asked what is it about you that allows you to survive this scorching heat and unrelenting environment to which the crab answered my skin and my legs for it pays to have thick skin if you can even call it that and you know what else when running sideways i surprise the likes of people like you consider the path of a falling leaf the distance in between the branch and the earth the slightest breeze could alter its course now consider yourself as that falling leaf falling falling and where did you come from and where are you now i'm not the face that looks into the camera saying yes this is my story see the scars the thickened skin i've lived a hard life i've survived you with the camera tell it to the world no that is not me i am the one off centered to the left or right and always out of focus for the sake of drama i am sometimes referred to as the forgotten one but you see that is not true i choose to sit in the corners of rooms you will not see my eyes most likely they are buried in a bowl of noodles i will smile occasionally but purely out of courtesy you probably smiled first and my stories i have none worth telling but even if i did for what it's worth i wouldn't tell you the smile i've concluded is a deceptive creature a creature born of necessity it disguises itself for wants and desires and rarely is it ever born of content of my time spent with k i did not crack a single smile that was until the awkward moment when addresses were exchanged and he said write me to which i paused then said i will

of spinning lies among truths a gift bestowed by a woman in a
dream her face like my mother's but distinctly not my mother
she was crossing the road with a bag of persimmons and in this
dream i was thirty two and driving a car a convertible red car
to make a long dream short she stepped directly into my path
all i saw were the persimmons flying one fell from the sky
splattered on my windshield another one landed on my lap
stained my khakis

you see back in the fifth grade i was labeled incorrigible old man
tanaka was not nice to begin with guarding his persimmons as
if they were sacred i mean what's the big deal it was only a fruit
i took but one or two well maybe three or four

my mother bought persimmons at a farm off the highway the man at the farm he said folks from around here don't eat these you know we give them to our horses do you have a horse my mother just smiled that familiar smile the one that conveyed she didn't speak english the same smile that told me she had just told him to fuck off she took the bag in one hand my wrist in the other we walked that path along the highway between us not a single word

or it will always be this way be it here or there yesterday or
tomorrow us or them it will always be this way you or i

· instructions ·

i take after my mother i don't measure or weigh or follow recipes when cooking i rely on intuition more often than not my intuition tells me to throw it out start over again

think long and hard he tells me chairs are made to go with
tables one slides right in to fit the other not always perfectly but
they fit none the less this act of being he refers to as a lifestyle
being the table being the chair are you sure he keeps asking as
i keep thinking long and hard

language manipulated becomes an equation resulting in a convoluted meaning this is a ploy on the part of the person lost for words on one of those humid nights in saigon we took refuge in a bar we shared a beer a glass of ice and i told k he was an enigma of a person rituals have a way of simplifying like watering the herb garden for exactly two hours she times herself from right to left then left to right this for her is a manageable life a bucket of water a hole punched ladle the scent of mint leaves her obsession with just the right shade of green

her hair remains a licorice black through two religions a lifetime
of incense unscented a rosary beaded broken rebeaded black as
redemption realized an afterthought of the father and the son
her delicate existence between and through black as defiance
subtle but sure of the lies kept truths discarded no one cares to
know that the gun concealed is always loaded that accidents
retraced to its very roots holds reason purpose that is to say
accidents are deliberate like her hair black as a color is absolute

after twenty years of waking at five working at six sleeping at eight her prescribed remedy was scripted in a catalog twenty years amounting to an engraved wall clock a gold plated watch a sapphire necklace the insignia like a brand of the three given a choice she chose the necklace for time she says holds little meaning she talks of stockholm going if she could during solstice where day is spent without the burden of night as it should be she says for a woman her age she stopped wearing watches no sense in looking for what's already known

three times a day as if ritualized it does not matter what it is
that we eat a bowl of white rice as the course not the filler what
matters is the act of eating together to reacquaint as family as
strangers to speak of the brother in that country of the other
of how in his world cooking with taro is new and exotic of how
at our table not there but here in the field in the house taro root
as a substitute is just another way as in eating together ritualized
three times a day

of the things i know however significant minor i file them away
to keep them with me always recipes in a tin box hidden behind
compartments comprising the heart some of these recipes i
return to often while others i file for just the sake of keeping
how the technique of holding chopsticks defines one's place in
the world or the image of my father combing my mother's hair
what i do not know i leave to the imagination one day i too will
find myself as my father or my mother my hair being combed
the hands of my lover searching for grays to uproot and discard
as for the unimaginable the recipe reads as follows *that which is*
beyond my imagination i will take comfort in not knowing

about discovery and the dumpster behind the supermarket the
stack of magazines with naked women of how in life there are
rules never spoken or written but learned deliberate like that
day i stood and walked for the first time this i hold on to when
in need of making sense even now i swear at the age of twenty
seven thirty five fifty four i could go to a dumpster in the heart
of suburbia in a brown paper bag and there it would be don't
ask why it's just that way that children learn of rules before
they learn of truth about discovery and the dumpster and the
stack of magazines hidden in the stack a magazine not for but
of men i need not say more for this is private is true is the truth
like beginnings and discoveries how they come in intervals
again and again

to find distance in the proximity of a step between the i and the self one step away from so that i may step back into this need to equate image to belief on my eighteenth birthday she gave me a rosary because i am will always be catholic

of this need to equate image to meaning on my twenty seventh
birthday she gave me a cross a detailed image devoid of
metaphors a man in pain his arms and feet nailed to beams
a scaled model to be worn in faith around one's neck because
i am that was all she would say

that which happens happens for a reason as in going to the movies on a friday afternoon the day of the test an in class essay on how hamlet relates to high school seniors five hundred words a prescription for life in a spanish dubbed theater where acting is chinese subtitles are in english the father dies so that the mother will teach reluctantly she teaches the son to fight the son grows up to exact revenge upon returning from my trip i called her to share of my experiences of drinking the blood of cobras diluted in a sweet rice wine of eating fruits the like of stars and dragons translated she said they were mythical fruits from a mythical land she could almost taste them on her tongue i spoke of meeting the relatives her sister-in-law who makes a living selling noodles on a good day she can make as much as fifty thousand dongs translated she said it equates to about four dollars a hard life but a life all the same i spoke of falling in love with the country and the people and of one particular man you would like him i told her he's quiet gentle and is a writer like myself translated she said she was late for church ours is a tonal language fifteen years a thousand miles countless attempts at telling this story how the meaning changes from father to son to sister to stranger for the record it was an accident that i am clear on a loaded gun a run away boy the need to uphold traditions in culture a camera at the funeral for pictures to send home and where did i fit in to claim such a story it was my eye that saw my hand that focused my camera that shot a phone call from your sister and what she said i still remember if you see him tell him to come home it was an accident the police say it was we want him to come home perhaps it is best that i leave it at this a futile attempt at telling the story returning to again and again like our names layered with reasons ours is a language embedded in tones to appease her mother she married a soldier a man twice her age but a man just the same to provide no less than what is necessary she would expect no more than the occasional visit while on leave away from the war a cordial smile a distant conversation the promise of returning whenever necessary with no love involved no bonds to break only the barest necessity of what is needed the comfort of knowing her mother was appeased and of her own daughter and what is expected to appease a mother in her old age no more no less than what is necessary

i would gladly share the apple that stems from this tree of
knowing heavy with the burden of being ripe of growing from
neglect resilient resistant to my hands extended cupped like a
ladle it carries water to quench your anger see how it drips
from the cracks of my fingers precious and fleeting see how it
cleanses this fruit unwanted of dust and conscience and
everything in between

first there is crying this is a given when executed with purpose the effects can be cathartic then there is eating because the crying can be draining someone tells a story then another then another then comes the laughter hysterical at times such is the recipe for a proper wake a proper life my mother called back ten minutes later to say that she was too late for church and that if i was happy then she too was happy because translated she is will always be my mother and i am will always be her son

· ruptures ·

to appease the self still finding comfort in of all things the
gravity of words i'll refer to these ruptures as antipoems

pardon the interruption but there is a scorpion a woman a frog and a ghost all wanting to come in they insist on entering into the book will this entity known as the other please step forward be it the frog the scorpion the ghost of my father is that you mother behind the disguise will the other please come forth at this time shed some light make sense of this book enter the sand crab from a previous poem he looks around examines his surroundings the page is a bit off it feels nothing like a poem the language he says is awkward and crude it is not fit for the likes of poetry he's not used to being stared at with such disdain the climate is too cold for even his thick skin he says you're a writer so write something beautiful something fluid write something to send me home enter the scorpion in a different time a different place why then is his story still the same he blames it on the writer this incessant need to be tragic it could have been it should have been a cliché of an ending happily ever after now is that so hard to write the other night i sat in a bar with three other people i'll call them carlito anna bartholemeu for no other reason than that of music the way these names fall from my tongue we were playing this game nonsensical in the moment profound in life we each asked a question we each gave an answer if you could be a character in a sitcom who would it be note for this question you must choose a character of the opposite gender if you could relive a single moment when would it be note for this question you can relive it only altering the past is not an option if you could live in any period what period what time for this question and this question only you must change your race your gender is optional if the world would end this time tomorrow what would you do today now note the answer to the last question we'll use as a starting point to begin the next round of nonsensical questions enter my mother playing the part of a mother though not my mother a mother nonetheless to authenticate her role she has died her teeth peppered her hair she has but one line of dialogue to deliver on cue her one chance to be someone other than my mother her one chance to speak completely out of character she receives her cue she clears her throat she says enough she exits the page

enter the ghost of my father dressed in a hawaiian patterned
short sleeved shirt bermuda shorts a straw brimmed hat i'm
leaving he says but before i go i leave you with a bit of advice
don't lose it he tells me don't lose it in translation well i'm off
he says i've got weeds to pull in those clouds

enter the frog speaking in his own defense for the record i did
not write these poems what do i know of love and of tragedy
what do i know of poetry what i do know i have always known
i am a toad this is my nature

enter k holding my words what you've written i cannot accept the truth as you have it is a figment a fragment at best what i consider to be true you fail to mention he returns the words he leaves the book

· endings ·

every word of every image is a step towards the end this
urgency dictates that the sentence as we know it no longer
an option grammar is obsolete stories once told in detailed
chapters have been reduced to a noun a verb the father dies the
lover leaves in search of his own ending perhaps now the
writing can finally begin

when looking for my father's grave site we asked that it be
beneath a tree in a lifetime of seeking refuge from country and
language and life itself he would have wanted it this way

that love could stem from the most remote corners of our imagination this is how things are and not of how it could or should be that is to say it is not enough that a fruit can be ugly but to also have it pickled for added sourness this is beyond the cruelest cruelty that is to say this is a story devoid of morals it can be told in the breath of a sentence the span of a lifetime that discretion is left to the one telling the story i am reverting to that voice not capable of telling stories in place of the narrative that voice takes on a child's declarative i am the father i am the son i am the lover i am i am the voice that existed before there were stories stories for the telling the voice that speaks in cryptic tongues the voice that insists on saying i love you and hearing it as i you love to end without ending on this preposition really i've tried to no avail for translated i am considered not whole of fragments and shards translated i am a shadow of in his memoir the young man wrote chapter after chapter without the use of punctuation his images bled from one the other his words were nomadic monks roaming the page having exhausted the stories of his young life the man decided he had arrived at an ending he wrote one last line nonchalantly he ended on a period when he woke the next morning he found the white pages void of print every life is a book the story scripted long before the first breath is taken that every book is a journey of learning and unlearning with each turn of the page that every journey is a language shrouded in silence

having traveled to that place you are reminded of me having
been reminded you call me on the phone having called we are
again here somewhere between words having found ourselves
somewhere between words we break the silence you say you've
been wanting you owe me this phone call to which i reply the
debt as of now is paid in full

four answers to a nonsensical question from four different characters i would pray i would fuck i would write a poem then fuck i would fuck then pray then write that fucking poem that the only true audience is the one not listening to know that i write despite of you the more i write the less you know to know that you i define as the reader this is all you need to know this is all i choose to tell

the other as perceived is language or the loss of other as place
stranger country beloved the other when deciphered is but the
self intently saying in loving you i lose myself

there is absolutely nothing poetic here to see nothing lyrical to hear go home to your families tell them you saw nothing forget what you thought you may have felt or touched language serves no purpose than that of meaning

PHOTO: Phu Tran

TRUONG TRAN was born in 1969 in Saigon, Vietnam. He and his family immigrated to the United States where they resettled in the San Francisco Bay Area. He received his undergraduate education at The University of California, Santa Cruz, and his MFA at San Francisco State University in creative writing. He is the recipient of poetry fellowships from the Arts Council of Santa Clara, The California Arts Council and The Creative Work Fund Grant. His poems have been published in numerous literary journals including *ZYZZYVA*, *The American Voice*, *Crazyhorse*, *Prairie Schooner*, *Poetry East*, *ACM (Another Chicago Magazine)* and *The North Dakota Quarterly*. Truong's first collection of poems, *The Book of Perceptions,* was a finalist for the Kiriyama Prize. His second collection, *placing the accents*, also published by Apogee Press, was a finalist for the Western States Book Award. Truong lives in San Francisco where he works as a copywriter.